WITHDRAWN

THE YEAR ONE

THE YEAR ONE

POEMS

BY

KATHLEEN RAINE

HAMISH HAMILTON
LONDON

First published in Great Britain 1952
by Hamish Hamilton Ltd
90 Great Russell St London WC1
Second Impression 1953

PRINTED IN GREAT BRITAIN
BY WESTERN PRINTING SERVICES LTD., BRISTOL

IN MEMORY
OF
HUMPHREY JENNINGS

Among those whom I wish to thank the first are Miss Helen Sutherland, in whose much-loved house more than a third of these poems were written; and Mr. John Hayward, for his kind and ruthless criticism. Acknowledgments are also due to *The Times Literary Supplement*, *The Listener*, *The New Statesman*, *World Review*, *Vogue*, *Botteghe Oscure*, *The New Yorker*, *Harper's Magazine*, *The Nation*, *Poetry* (Chicago) and *The Trifler*, in which many of these poems were first published.

CONTENTS

NORTHUMBRIAN SEQUENCE

So seems the life of man, O King, as a sparrow's flight through the hall when you are sitting at meat in winter-tide, the fire on the hearth, the icy rainstorm without.

The sparrow flies in at one door and tarries for a moment in the light and heat of the hearth-fire, then flies forth into the darkness whence it came.—*Words attributed to an ealdorman, in Bede's account of the conversion of Eadwine, King of Northumberland.*

I

Pure I was before the world began,
I was the violence of wind and wave,
I was the bird before bird ever sang.

I was never still,
I turned upon the axis of my joy,
I was the lonely dancer on the hill.

The rain upon the mountainside,
The rising mist,
I was the sea's unrest.

I wove the web of colour
Before the rainbow,
The intricacy of the flower
Before the leaf grew.

I was the buried ore,
The fossil forest,
I knew the roots of things:
Before death's kingdom
I passed through the grave.

Times out of mind my journey
Circles the universe
And I remain
Before the first day.

II

Him I praise with my mute mouth of night
Uttering silences until the stars
Hang at the still nodes of my troubled waves.
Into my dark I have drawn down his light.

I weave upon the empty floor of space
The bridal dance, I dance the mysteries
That set the house of Pentheus ablaze.
His radiance shines into my darkest place.

He lays in my deep grave his deathless fires,
In me his flame springs fountain tree and heart,
Soars up from nature's bed in a bird's flight.
Into my dark I have drawn down his light.

My leaves draw down the sun with their green
   hands
And bind his rays into the world's wild rose.
I hold my mirroring seas before his face.
His radiance shines into my darkest place.

See, the clear sky is threaded with a thousand rays,
The birds' unseen but certain ways
That draw the swallow and the homing dove
As eyebeams overleap distances between stars.

Whistle of wings heralds oncoming spirit—
Life-bearing birds follow the bright invisible trace
That draws the skein of grey geese flying north
Or hangs the hawk at one point, motionless.
Life's ways pass through us, over us, beyond us.

Birds home to the house of the world, to the islands,
To ledges of sheer cliff, to wind-tossed tree-tops
To the high moorland where the lapwing builds:
Nest and grave are where the quick joy fails.

Their great and certain impulses are spent
In snowdrift, salt wave, dashed against rock-face,
But strong winds buffeted by wind and blizzard
Still follow the way that leads through storm to rest.

Bird angels, heavenly vehicles,
They die and are reborn—the bird is dust
But the deathless winged delight pursues its way.

Shining travellers from another dimension
Whose heaven-sent flight homes to the green earth,
What gossamer desire floats out to guide
Spirit ascending and descending between grave and sky?

IV

Let in the wind
Let in the rain
Let in the moors tonight,

The storm beats on my window-pane,
Night stands at my bed-foot,
Let in the fear,
Let in the pain,
Let in the trees that toss and groan,
Let in the north tonight.

Let in the nameless formless power
That beats upon my door,
Let in the ice, let in the snow,
The banshee howling on the moor,
The bracken-bush on the bleak hillside,
Let in the dead tonight.

The whistling ghost behind the dyke,
The dead that rot in mire,
Let in the thronging ancestors
The unfulfilled desire,
Let in the wraith of the dead earl,
Let in the unborn tonight.

Let in the cold,
Let in the wet,
Let in the loneliness,
Let in the quick,
Let in the dead,
Let in the unpeopled skies.

Oh how can virgin fingers weave
A covering for the void,
How can my fearful heart conceive
Gigantic solitude?
How can a house so small contain
A company so great?
Let in the dark,
Let in the dead,
Let in your love tonight.

Let in the snow that numbs the grave,
Let in the acorn-tree,
The mountain stream and mountain stone,
Let in the bitter sea.

Fearful is my virgin heart
And frail my virgin form,
And must I then take pity on
The raging of the storm
That rose up from the great abyss
Before the earth was made,
That pours the stars in cataracts
And shakes this violent world?

Let in the fire,
Let in the power,
Let in the invading might.

Gentle must my fingers be
And pitiful my heart
Since I must bind in human form
A living power so great,
A living impulse great and wild

That cries about my house
With all the violence of desire
Desiring this my peace.

Pitiful my heart must hold
The lonely stars at rest,
Have pity on the raven's cry
The torrent and the eagle's wing,
The icy water of the tarn
And on the biting blast.

Let in the wound,
Let in the pain,
Let in your child tonight.

V

The sleeper at the rowan's foot
Dreams the darkness at the root,
Dreams the flow that ascends the vein
And fills with world the dreamer's brain.

Wild tree filled with wind and rain
Day and night invade your dream,
Unseen brightness of the sun,
Waters flowing underground
Rise in bud and flower and shoot;
And the burden is so great
Of the dark flow from without,
Of sun streaming from the sky
And the dead rising from the root,
Of the earth's desire to be
In this dreaming incarnate
That world has overflowed the tree.

Oh do not wake, oh do not wake
The sleeper in the rowan's shade,
Mountains rest within his thought,
Clouds are drifting in his brain,
Snows upon his eyelids fall,
Winds are piping in his song,
Night is gathered at his root,
Stars are blossoming in his crown,
Storm without finds peace within,
World is resting in his dream.

Lonely dreamer on the hill
I have dreamed a thousand years,
I have dreamed returning spring,
Earth's delight and golden sun,
I have dreamed the pheasant's eye,
The heather and the flashing burn,
For the world has filled my dream:
Dream has overflowed the tree.

World without presses so sore
Upon the roots and branches fine
The dreamer can contain no more
And overflows in falling flowers,
Lets fall the bitter rowan fruit
Harsh as tears and bright as blood,
Berries that the wild birds eat
Till stripped of dream the sleeper lies,
Stripped of world the naked tree.
But on the hillside I have heard
The voice of the prophetic bird
That feeds upon the bitter fruit,
I have heard the blackbird sing
The wild music of the wind,
Utter the note the sun would cry,
Sing for the burn that flows away.

The sleeper of the rowan tree
As full of earth as dream can know,
As full of dream as tree can bear
Sends the bird singing in the air
As full of world as song can cry,
And yet the song is overflowed,
For pressing at the tree's deep root
Still underground, unformed, is world.

The invading world must break the dream
So heavy is the weight of sky,
So violent the water's flow
So vast the hills that would be born,
Beyond the utterance of bird
The mountain voice that would be sung,
The world of wild that would be man:
The dream has overflowed the tree.

The window-panes grow dark, the walls recede,
Grow infinitely remote, and the familiar room
No longer houses me, no longer encloses;
House insubstantial into nothing dwindles,
I and the earth must part—and who am I
That with this dark winged messenger must fly
Into the soul's dark night?

I—who am I, that enter death's dimension?
I and this swift-winged bird-form have grown one,
My thought is fused with his thought, will with his
    will,
And we are one in purposes unknown
To bird or soul, human or angel mind,
And yet we go—the destination draws us.

As sleeper wakes from sleep, I wake from waking.
World's image fails and founders, mountain forms,
Garden and trees, heel over into darkness,
Go down the night like ice in northern ocean,
Nothing withholds house from crumbling, hills from
    falling.
Only the bird-flight, and this travelling
Of the soul into its own night, are certain.

House that has sheltered me since I was born,
Flowers and trees and skies and running burn,
Body of death I lifelong have been building,
My face, hands, voice, language and cast of thought
No longer me, or mine—I dreamed them into being,
Being that is unmade again into the night,
Grows tenuous, and is gone.

In the round barrow on the moor, a king's sword
    rusts
Under the cropped turf; necklace and golden cup
Lie in the finer dust of a dead queen,
And when the ghosts come blowing on the north
    wind
They find again the treasures that once seemed
Inseparable from their own living, underground
In the earth circle, in the bone's mound.

I too have haunted memories,
Places once loved, travelled back thirty years
To where home was, to find the hills still standing
To find the old stone house, the trees cut down,
But water still flowing from the village well
Where once I dipped my bucket as a child.
Even such returning desecrates—
Do not disturb the barrow on the hill,
Leave buried there the treasure of past days.

Not in overlong continuance see
Of amulet or ghost, in wraith of what has been,
Evidence of soul's immortality.
The ghost that haunts, the haunting memory
Is the continuance only of the dead.
Such earth-bound spirits, into soul's night unborn
Miss the one way to that destination
From which the homing soul knows no return.

Yet with what infinite gentleness being flows
Into the forms of nature, and unfolds
Into the slowly ascending tree of life
That opens, bud by bud, into the sky.
World, with what unending patience, grows,
Ascends the roots from the dark well of night
From stone to plant, from blind sense into sight
Up to the highest branch, where the raven head
        grows white.

But body was imperfect from the first,
Heart, sense, and the fine mesh of word and thought
Will not contain the abundance of the world.
The god that in the ascending tree, bird, stone,
River and mountain, wind and rain
Has remained hidden since the world began,
The power that overflows and shatters every form,
Calls on death to come, to break the imperfect
        mould.

Spirit, freed from the form into which you flowed,
Prisoned merlin of the groaning tree,
The self you were in nature falls away
All at once into dust, as the bird-heart homes.
Dark into dark, spirit into spirit flies,
Home, with not one dear image in the heart.

LOVE SPELL

By the travelling wind
By the restless clouds
By the space of the sky,

By the foam of the surf
By the curve of the wave
By the flowing of the tide,

By the way of the sun,
By the dazzle of light
By the path across the sea,
                    Bring my lover.

By the way of the air,
By the hoodie crow's flight
By the eagle on the wind,

By the cormorant's cliff
By the seal's rock
By the raven's crag,

By the shells on the strand
By the ripples on the sand
By the brown sea-wrack,
                    Bring my lover.

By the mist and the rain
By the waterfall
By the running burn,

By the clear spring
By the holy well
And the fern by the pool
          Bring my lover.

By the sheepwalks on the hills
By the rabbit's tracks
By the stones of the ford,
          Bring my lover.

By the long shadow
By the evening light
By the midsummer sun
          Bring my lover.

By the scent of the white rose
Of the bog myrtle
And the scent of the thyme
          Bring my lover.

By the lark's song
By the blackbird's note
By the raven's croak
          Bring my lover.

By the voices of the air
By the water's song
By the song of a woman
          Bring my lover.

By the sticks burning on the hearth
By the candle's flame
By the fire in the blood
          Bring my lover.

By the touch of hands
By the meeting of lips
By love's unrest
         Bring my lover.

By the quiet of the night
By the whiteness of my breast
By the peace of sleep
         Bring my lover.

By the blessing of the dark
By the beating of the heart
By my unborn child,
         Bring my lover.

SPELL AGAINST SORROW

Who will take away
Carry away sorrow,
Bear away grief?

Stream wash away
Float away sorrow,
Flow away, bear away
Wear away sorrow,
Carry away grief.

Mists hide away
Shroud my sorrow,
Cover the mountains,
Overcloud remembrance,
Hide away grief.

Earth take away
Make away sorrow,
Bury the lark's bones
Under the turf.
Bury my grief.

Black crow tear away
Rend away sorrow,
Talon and beak
Pluck out the heart
And the nerves of pain,
Tear away grief.

Sun take away
Melt away sorrow,
Dew lies grey,
Rain hangs on the grass,
Sun dry tears.

Sleep take away
Make away sorrow,
Take away the time,
Fade away place,
Carry me away
From the world of my sorrow.

Song sigh away
Breathe away sorrow,
Words tell away,
Spell away sorrow,
Charm away grief.

SPELL TO BRING LOST
CREATURES HOME

Home, home,
Wild birds home!
Lark to the grass,
Wren to the hedge,
Rooks to the tree-tops,
Swallow to the eaves,
Eagle to its crag
And raven to its stone,
All birds home!

Home, home,
Strayed ones home,
Rabbit to burrow
Fox to earth,
Mouse to the wainscot,
Rat to the barn,
Cattle to the byre,
Dog to the hearth,
All beasts home!

Home, home,
Wanderers home,
Cormorant to rock
Gulls from the storm,
Boat to the harbour
Safe sail home!

Children home,
At evening home,
Boys and girls
From the roads come home,
Out of the rain
Sons come home,
From the gathering dusk,
Young ones home!

Home, home,
All souls home,
Dead to the graveyard,
Living to the lamplight,
Old to the fireside,
Girls from the twilight,
Babe to the breast
And heart to its haven,
Lost ones home!

SPELL OF CREATION

Within the flower there lies a seed,
Within the seed there springs a tree,
Within the tree there spreads a wood.

In the wood there burns a fire,
And in the fire there melts a stone,
Within the stone a ring of iron.

Within the ring there lies an O
Within the O there looks an eye,
In the eye there swims a sea,

And in the sea reflected sky,
And in the sky there shines the sun,
Within the sun a bird of gold.

Within the bird there beats a heart,
And from the heart there flows a song,
And in the song there sings a word.

In the word there speaks a world,
A word of joy, a world of grief,
From joy and grief there springs my love.

Oh love, my love, there springs a world,
And on the world there shines a sun
And in the sun there burns a fire,

Within the fire consumes my heart
And in my heart there beats a bird,
And in the bird there wakes an eye,

Within the eye, earth, sea and sky,
Earth, sky and sea within an O
Lie like the seed within the flower.

THE UNLOVED

I am pure loneliness
I am empty air
I am drifting cloud.

I have no form
I am boundless
I have no rest.

I have no house
I pass through places
I am indifferent wind.

I am the white bird
Flying away from land
I am the horizon.

I am a wave
That will never reach the shore

I am an empty shell
Cast up on the sand.

I am the moonlight
On the cottage with no roof.

I am the forgotten dead
In the broken vault on the hill.

I am the old man
Carrying his water in a pail.

I am light
Travelling in empty space.

I am a diminishing star
Speeding away
Out of the universe.

Because I love
> The sun pours out its rays of living gold
> Pours out its gold and silver on the sea.

Because I love
> The earth upon her astral spindle winds
> Her ecstasy-producing dance.

Because I love
> Clouds travel on the winds through wide skies,
> Skies wide and beautiful, blue and deep.

Because I love
> Wind blows white sails,
> The wind blows over flowers, the sweet wind
> blows.

Because I love
> The ferns grow green, and green the grass, and
> green
> The transparent sunlit trees.

Because I love
> Larks rise up from the grass
> And all the leaves are full of singing birds.

Because I love
> The summer air quivers with a thousand wings,
> Myriads of jewelled eyes burn in the light.

Because I love
>The iridescent shells upon the sand
Take forms as fine and intricate as thought.

Because I love
>There is an invisible way across the sky,
Birds travel by that way, the sun and moon
And all the stars travel that path by night.

Because I love
>There is a river flowing all night long.

Because I love
>All night the river flows into my sleep,
Ten thousand living things are sleeping in my
>arms,
And sleeping wake, and flowing are at rest.

Let him be safe in sleep
As leaves folded together
As young birds under wings
As the unopened flower.

Let him be hidden in sleep
As islands under rain,
As mountains within their clouds,
As hills in the mantle of dusk.

Let him be free in sleep
As the flowing tides of the sea,
As the travelling wind on the moor,
As the journeying stars in space.

Let him be upheld in sleep
As a cloud at rest on the air,
As sea-wrack under the waves
When the flowing tide covers all
And the shells' delicate lives
Open on the sea-floor.

Let him be healed in sleep
In the quiet waters of night
In the mirroring pool of dreams
Where memory returns in peace,
Where the troubled spirit grows wise
And the heart is comforted.

SPELL OF SAFEKEEPING

Wings over nest
Shelter and hide
From mouths of night,

Rose with green
Calyx enclose
From storm and rain,

Lid over eye,
Intangible dream,
Cover the sky.

Arms enfold
Lover and child,
Safe withhold
Flesh and blood
From dread of dark
And death by day.

TWO INVOCATIONS OF DEATH

I

Death, I repent
Of these hands and feet
That for forty years
Have been my own
And I repent
Of flesh and bone,
Of heart and liver,
Of hair and skin—
Rid me, death,
Of face and form,
Of all that I am.

And I repent
Of the forms of thought,
The habit of mind
And heart crippled
By long-spent pain,
The memory-traces
Faded and worn
Of vanished places
And human faces
Not rightly seen
Or understood,
Rid me, death,
Of the words I have used.

Not this or that
But all is amiss,
That I have done,
And I have seen
Sin and sorrow
Befoul the world—
Release me, death,
Forgive, remove
From place and time
The trace of all
That I have been.

From a place I came
That was never in time,
From the beat of a heart
That was never in pain.
The sun and the moon,
The wind and the world,
The song and the bird
Travelled my thought
Time out of mind.
Shall I know at last
My lost delight?

Tell me, death,
How long must I sorrow
My own sorrow?
While I remain
The world is ending,
Forests are falling,
Suns are fading,
While I am here
Now is ending
And in my arms
The living are dying.
Shall I come at last
To the lost beginning?

Words and words
Pour through my mind
Like sand in the shell
Of the ear's labyrinth,
The desert of brain's
Cities and solitudes,
Dreams, speculations
And vast forgetfulness.
Shall I learn at last
The lost meaning?

Oh my lost love
I have seen you fly
Away like a bird,
As a fish elude me,
A stone ignore me,
In a tree's maze
You have closed against me
The spaces of earth,
Prolonged to the stars'
Infinite distances,
With strange eyes
You have not known me,
Thorn you have wounded,
Fire you have burned
And talons torn me.
How long must I bear
Self and identity—
Shall I find at last
My lost being?

MESSAGE

Look, beloved child, into my eyes, see there
Your self, mirrored in that living water
From whose deep pools all images of earth are born.
See, in the gaze that holds you dear
All that you were, are, and shall be for ever.
In recognition beyond time and seeming
Love knows the face that each soul turns towards
      heaven.

LAMENT

Where are those dazzling hills touched by the sun,
Those crags in childhood that I used to climb?
Hidden, hidden under mist is yonder mountain,
Hidden is the heart.

A day of cloud, a lifetime falls between,
Gone are the heather moors and the pure stream,
Gone are the rocky places and the green,
Hidden, hidden under sorrow is yonder mountain.

Oh storm and gale of tears, whose blinding screen
Makes weather of grief, snow's drifting curtain
Palls the immortal heights once seen.
Hidden is the heart.

A WORD KNOWN TO THE DEAD

I watch white hills grow pale as empty air,
Cold draught of space blows the drifting snow,
The grey stone boundaries fade, and the sun darkens.

I watch an ash-tree stand bared to the sky
As void of being as the invisible air
That cannot bind or bend the rainbow from the
    darkness.

Winter how many birds' bright eyes has frozen
Into a dark gaze, and dead wild creatures stare
With open eyes upon the dazzling hills,
Eyes vacant as interstellar space, where light is dark-
    ness.

Tree's branches faint and flicker from the eye,
There is no road, earth fails beneath my feet
And the hardest rock in the hills is hollow as night,

For I have heard
A certain cold word spoken in the heart,
A word that the dead hear and obey in darkness.

THREE POEMS ON ILLUSION

I

The Mirage

No, I have seen the mirage tremble, seen how thin
The veil stretched over apparent time and space
To make the habitable earth, the enclosed garden.

I saw on a bare hillside an ash-tree stand
And all its intricate branches suddenly
Failed, as I gazed, to be a tree,
And road and hillside failed to make a world.
Hill, tree, sky, distance, only seemed to be
And I saw nothing I could give a name,
Not any name known to the heart.

What failed? The retina received
The differing waves of light, or rays of darkness,
Eyes, hands, all senses brought me
Messages that lifelong I had believed.
Appearances that once composed reality
Here turned to dust, to mist, to motes in the eye
Or like the reflection broken on a pool
The unrelated visual fragments foundered
On a commotion of those deeps
Where earth floats safe, when waves are still.

The living instrument
When fingers gently touch the strings,
Or when a quiet wind
Blows through the reed, makes music of birds,

Song, words, the human voice.
Too strong a blast from outer space,
A blow too heavy breaks and silences
The singer and the song;
A grief too violent
Wrecks the image of the world, on waves whose
    amplitude
Beats beyond the compass of the heart.

The waves subside, the image reassembles:
There was a tree once more, hills, and the world,
But I have seen the emptiness of air
Ready to swallow up the bird in its flight,
Or note of music, or winged word, the void
That traps the rabbit on cropped turf as in a snare,
Lies at the heart of the wren's warm living eggs,
In pollen dust of summer flowers, opens
Within the smallest seed of grass, the abyss
That now and always underlies the hills.

II

The Instrument

Death, and it is broken,
The delicate apparatus of the mind,
Tactile, sensitive to light, responsive to sound,
The soul's instrument, tuned to earth's music,
Vibrant to all the waves that break on the shores of
     the world.

Perhaps soul only puts out a hand,
Antenna or pseudopodium, an extended touch
To receive the spectrum of colour, and the lower
     octave of pain,
Reaches down into the waves of nature
As a child dips an arm into the sea,
And death is the withdrawal of attention
That has discovered all it needs to know,
Or, if not all, enough for now,
If not enough, something to bear in mind.

And it may be that soul extends
Organs of sense
Tuned to waves here scarcely heard, or only
Heard distantly in dreams,
Worlds other otherwise than as stars,
Asteroids and suns are distant, in natural space.
The supersonic voices of angels reach us
Even how, and we touch one another
Sometimes, in love, with hands that are not hands,
With immaterial substance, with a body
Of interfusing thought, a living eye,
Spirit that passes unhindered through walls of stone
And walks upon those waves that we call ocean.

III

Exile

Then, I had no doubt
That snowdrops, violets, all creatures, I myself
Were lovely, were loved, were love.
Look, they said,
And I had only to look deep into the heart,
Dark, deep into the violet, and there read,
Before I knew of any word for flower or love,
The flower, the love, the word.

They never wearied of telling their being; and I
Asked of the rose, only more rose, the violet
More violet; untouched by time
No flower withered or flame died,
But poised in its own eternity, until the looker moved
On to another flower, opening its entity.

I see them now across a void
Wider and deeper than time and space.
All that I have come to be
Lies between my heart and the rose,
The flame, the bird, the blade of grass.
The flowers are veiled;
And in a shadow-world, appearances
Pass across a great *toile vide*
Where the image flickers, vanishes,
Where nothing is, but only seems.
But still the mind, curious to pursue
Long followed them, as they withdrew
Deep within their inner distances,

Pulled the petals from flowers, the wings from flies,
Hunted the heart with a dissecting-knife
And scattered under a lens the dust of life;
But the remoter, stranger
Scales iridescent, cells, spindles, chromosomes,
Still merely are:
With hail, snow-crystals, mountains, stars,
Fox in the dusk, lightning, gnats in the evening air
They share the natural mystery,
Proclaim I AM, and remain nameless.

Sometimes from far away
They sign to me;
A violet smiles from the dim verge of darkness,
A raindrop hangs beckoning on the eaves,
And once, in long wet grass,
A young bird looked at me.
Their being is lovely, is love;
And if my love could cross the desert self
That lies between all that I am and all that is,
They would forgive and bless.

Face of the long-dead
Floating up from under the deep waves
Of time, that we try to see,
To draw towards us by closer looking, that fades
And will not become more clear than shadow,
Mist gathering always like dusk round a dead king,
That face, however closely we look, is always depart-
    ing,
Neither questions nor answers us. It is still,
It is whole, has known, loved, suffered all,
And un-known all again.
That face of man
Un-knows us now; whatever being passed
Beyond that holy shroud into the mind of God
No longer sees this earth: we are alone.

THREE POEMS OF INCARNATION

I

At the day's end I found

Nightfall wrapped about a stone.

I took the cold stone in my hand,
The shadowy surfaces of life unwound,
And within I found
A bird's fine bone.

I warmed the relic in my hand
Until a living heart
Beat, and the tides flowed
Above, below, within.

There came a boat riding the storm of blood
And in the boat a child,

In the boat a child
Riding the waves of song,
Riding the waves of pain.

Invocation

Child in the little boat
Come to the land
Child of the seals
Calf of the whale
Spawn of the octopus
Fledgeling of cormorant
Gannet and herring-gull,
Come from the sea,
Child of the sun,
Son of the sky.

Safely pass
The mouths of the water,
The mouths of night,
The teeth of the rocks,
The mouths of the wind,
Safely float
On the dangerous waves
Of an ocean sounding
Deeper than red
Darker than violet,
Safely cross
The ground-swell of pain
Of the waves that break
On the shores of the world.

Life everlasting
Love has prepared
The paths of your coming.
Plankton and nekton
Free-swimming pelagic
Spawn of the waters
Has brought you to birth
In the life-giving pools,
Spring has led you
Over the meadows
In fox's fur
Has nestled and warmed you,
With the houseless hare
In the rushes has sheltered
Warm under feathers
Of brooding wings
Safe has hidden
In the grass secretly
Clothed in disguise
Of beetle and grasshopper
Small has laid you
Under a stone
In the nest of the ants
Myriadfold scattered
In pollen of pine forests
Set you afloat
Like dust on the air
And winged in multitudes
Hatched by the sun
From the mud of rivers.

Newborn you have lain
In the arms of mothers,
You have drawn life
From a myriad breasts,
The mating of animals
Has not appalled you,
The longing of lovers
You have not betrayed,
You have come unscathed
From the field of battle
From famine and plague
You have lived undefiled
In the gutters of cities
We have seen you dancing
Barefoot in villages
You have been to school.
But kept your wisdom.

Child in the little boat,
Come to the land,
Child of the seals.

III

Who stands at my door in the storm and rain
On the threshold of being?
One who waits till you call him in
From the empty night.

Are you a stranger, out in the storm,
Or has my enemy found me out
On the edge of being?

I am no stranger who stands at the door
Nor enemy come in the secret night,
I am your child, in darkness and fear
On the verge of being.

Go back, my child, to the rain and the storm,
For in this house there is sorrow and pain
In the lonely night.

I will not go back for sorrow or pain,
For my true love weeps within
And waits for my coming.

Go back, my babe, to the vacant night
For in this house dwell sin and hate
On the verge of being.

I will not go back for hate or sin,
I will not go back for sorrow or pain,
For my true love mourns within
On the threshold of night.

THE VICTIMS

FOR G.M.

They walk towards us willingly and gently,
Unblemished, the white kid, the calf,
Their newborn coats scarcely dry from the natal
    waters.
Each hair lies in its new place, ripple-marked
By the rhythms of growth, the tides
That washed them up onto the shores of time.

Their young eyes, unsurprised, look towards us,
We see them stand, beautiful, on spring grass
Knowing that the upgathering of perfect form must
    pass,
Those intricate knots of ganglia and veins,
The rhythmic heart, the breath of life.
We first receive their wounding in our hearts
With all the inexpressible guilt of love;
For the first worshipping touch of our tragic hands
    must soil
And trouble the unconscious unicorn
That does not even know it stands on earth.
We offer them bunches of buttercups and spring
    grass
With all the inexpressible love of guilt:
We strike, even as we look,
The first wound of sacrifice.

THE COMPANY

So many gathered in my room last night.
I felt them close all round me, existences,
Living presences, invisible essences,
Each centred in its own peculiar secret joy,
Each joy given being by a peculiar wisdom
Pertaining to its nature like a dimension,
Or like a world, enclosed within a spirit,
But none a spirit enclosed within a world.

Not in the world, and yet they gathered in my room;
Some stood still, inside the door, some
Thronged the firelight and the shadows; some hung
Like resting birds, in the curtains, perched high
On the bookshelves, poised on the opening flowers
Of a hyacinth, others hid in their own fiery darkness.

Where had they come from?
Out of my joy, out of my sorrow,
Living entities sprung into life from the dust
Of my existence, taking wing, making song?
Or were they there already before I came
Alone into my room, waiting
Until my joy should open eyes to see them,
Until my sorrow should reach down
Into the depths of being, and there find them,
Find such a company of living multitude?

THIS BODY OF DEATH

Forgiven and made pure, what of all this
Self could remain?
This person formed
For sin, by sin?
How could these hands be mine,
Shaped as they are by all the ill I have done,
Life of creatures taken,
Blows given, delicate things broken,
Struck violently, green textures torn,
Another living being touched ungently—
Shaped as they are by all life's restless cruelty,
Forgiven, these hands must die.

Forgiven, how could this face
That fear and coldness,
Unloving blindness, anxious weariness
Have marked and lined,
These features formed and framed
By trivial indifference,
Unstable pettiness and latent violence,
How could this face be blessed,
Bearing its record of a life lived amiss?

Each creature is the signature of its action.
The gull swoops, shaped by wind and hunger,
Eyes and scavenging beak, and strong white wings
Turned to a fine edge of beauty and power by wind
    and water.
Scream and wing-beat utter the holy truth of its being.
Man acts amiss: pure only the song
That breaks from the lips of love, or the wordless cry
When grief or pain makes mock of all that is human
    in us.

Passive I lie, looking up through leaves,
An eye only, one of the eyes of earth
That open at a myriad points at the living surface.
Eyes that earth opens see and delight
Because of the leaves, because of the unfolding of the
    leaves.
The folding, veining, imbrication, fluttering, resting,
The green and deepening manifold of the leaves.

Eyes of the earth know only delight
Untroubled by anything that I am, and I am
    nothing:
All that nature is, receive and recognize,
Pleased with the sky, the falling water and the
    flowers,
With bird and fish and the striations of stone.
Every natural form, living and moving
Delights these eyes that are no longer mine
That open upon earth and sky pure vision.
Nature sees, sees itself, is both seer and seen.

This is the divine repose, that watches
The ever-changing light and shadow, rock and sky
    and ocean.

THE MARRIAGE OF PSYCHE

1. *The House*

In my love's house
There are hills and pastures carpeted with flowers,
His roof is the blue sky, his lamp the evening star,
The doors of his house are the winds, and the rain
    his curtain.
In his house are many mountains, each alone,
And islands where the sea-birds home.

In my love's house
There is a waterfall that flows all night
Down from the mountain summit where the snow
    lies
White in the shimmering blue of everlasting summer,
Down from the high crag where the eagle flies.
At his threshold the tides of ocean rise,
And the porpoise follows the shoals into still bays
Where starfish gleam on brown weed under still
    water.

In sleep I was borne here
And waking found rivers and waves my servants,
Sun and cloud and winds, bird-messengers,
And all the flocks of his hills and shoals of his seas.
I rest, in the heat of the day, in the light shadow of
    leaves
And voices of air and water speak to me.
All this he has given me, whose face I have never
    seen,
But into whose all-enfolding arms I sink in sleep.

2. *The Ring*

He has married me with a ring, a ring of bright water
Whose ripples travel from the heart of the sea,
He has married me with a ring of light, the glitter
Broadcast on the swift river.
He has married me with the sun's circle
Too dazzling to see, traced in summer sky.
He has crowned me with the wreath of white cloud
That gathers on the snowy summit of the mountain,
Ringed me round with the world-circling wind,
Bound me to the whirlwind's centre.
He has married me with the orbit of the moon
And with the boundless circle of the stars,
With the orbits that measure years, months, days and
    nights,
Set the tides flowing,
Command the winds to travel or be at rest.

At the ring's centre,
Spirit, or angel troubling the still pool,
Causality not in nature,
Finger's touch that summons at a point, a moment
Stars and planets, life and light
Or gathers cloud about an apex of cold,
Transcendent touch of love summons my world to
    being.

SHELLS

Reaching down arm-deep into bright water
I gathered on white sand under waves
Shells, drifted up on beaches where I alone
Inhabit a finite world of years and days.
I reached my arm down a myriad years
To gather treasure from the yester-millennial sea-
floor,
Held in my fingers forms shaped on the day of
creation.

Building their beauty in the three dimensions
Over which the world recedes away from us,
And in the fourth, that takes away ourselves
From moment to moment and from year to year
From first to last they remain in their continuous
present.
The helix revolves like a timeless thought,
Instantaneous from apex to rim
Like a dance whose figure is limpet or murex, cowrie
or golden winkle.

They sleep on the ocean floor like humming-tops
Whose music is the mother-of-pearl octave of the
rainbow,
Harmonious shells that whisper for ever in our ears,
'The world that you inhabit has not yet been
created.'

ROCK

There is stone in me that knows stone,
Substance of rock that remembers the unending un-
    ending
Simplicity of rest
While scorching suns and ice ages
Pass over rock-face swiftly as days.
In the longest time of all come the rock's changes,
Slowest of all rhythms, the pulsations
That raise from the planet's core the mountain
    ranges
And weather them down to sand on the sea-floor.

Remains in me record of rock's duration.
My ephemeral substance was still in the veins of the
    earth from the beginning,
Patient for its release, not questioning
When, when will come the flowering, the flowing,
The pulsing, the awakening, the taking wing,
The long longed-for night of the bridegroom's
    coming.

There is stone in me that knows stone,
Whose sole state is stasis
While the slow cycle of the stars whirls a world of
    rock
Through light-years where in nightmare I fall crying
' Must I travel fathomless distance for ever and
    ever? '
All that is in me of the rock, replies
' For ever, if it must be: be, and be still; endure.'

WATER

There is a stream that flowed before the first begin-
　　ning
Of bounding form that circumscribes
Protophyte and protozoon.
The passive permeable sea obeys,
Reflects, rises and falls as forces of moon and wind
Draw this way or that its weight of waves;
But the mutable water holds no trace
Of crest or ripple or whirlpool; the wave breaks,
Scatters in a thousand instantaneous drops
That fall in sphere and ovoid, film-spun bubbles
Upheld in momentary equilibrium of strain and
　　stress
In the ever-changing network woven between stars.

When, in the flux, the first bounding membrane
Forms, like the memory-trace of a preceding state,
When the linked organic chain
Holds against current and tide its microcosm,
Of man's first disobedience, what first cause
Impresses with inherent being
Entities, selves, globules, vase-shapes, vortices,
Amoeboid, ovoid, pulsing or ciliate,
That check the flow of waters like forms of thought,
Pause, poised in the unremembering current
By what will to be fathered in the primal matrix?
The delicate tissue of life retains, bears
The stigmata, the trace, the signature, endures
The tension of the formative moment, withstands
The passive downward deathward streaming.
Leaps the falls, a salmon ascending, a tree growing.

But still the stream that flows down to stillness
Seeks the end-all of all waters,
Welcomes all solving, dissolving, undoing,
Returns, loses itself, loses self and bounds,
Body, identity, memory, sinks to forgetfulness,
The state of unknowing, unbeing,
The flux that precedes all life, that we reassume, dying,
Ceasing to trouble the flowing of things with the fleeting
Dream and hope and despair of this transient perilous selving.

INTROSPECTION

If you go deep
Into the heart
What do you find there?
Fear, fear,
Fear of the jaws of the rock,
Fear of the teeth and splinters of iron that tear
Flesh from the bone, and the moist
Blood, running unfelt
From the wound, and the hand
Suddenly moist and red.

If you go deep
Into the heart
What do you find?
Grief, grief,
Grief for the life unlived,
For the loves unloved,
For the child never now to be born,
The unbidden anguish, when the fair moon
Rises over still summer seas, and the pain
Of sunlight scattered in vain on spring grass.

If you go deeper
Into the heart
What do you find there?
Death, death,
Death that lets all go by,
Lets the blood flow from the wound,
Lets the night pass,
Endures the day with indifference, knowing that all
    must end.

Sorrow is not for ever, and sense
Endures no extremities,
Death is the last
Secret implicit within you, the hidden, the deepest
Knowledge of all you will ever unfold
In this body of earth.

THE MOMENT

Never, never again
This moment, never
These slow ripples
Across smooth water,
Never again these
Clouds white and grey
In sky sharp crystalline
Blue as the tern's cry
Shrill in light air
Salt from the ocean,
Sweet from flowers.

Here coincide
The long histories
Of forms recurrent
That meet at a point
And part in a moment,
The rapid waves
Of wind and water
And slower rhythm
Of rock weathering
And land sinking.

In teeming pools
The life cycle
Of brown weed
Is intersecting
The frequencies
Of diverse shells
Each with its variant

Arc or spiral
Spun from a point
In tone and semitone
Of formal octave.

Here come soaring
White gulls
Leisurely wheeling
In air over islands
Sea pinks and salt grass,
Gannet and eider,
Curlew and cormorant
Each a differing
Pattern of ecstasy
Recurring at nodes
In an on-flowing current,
The perpetual species,
Repeated, renewed
By the will of joy
In eggs lodged safe
On perilous ledges.

The sun that rises
Upon one earth
Sets on another.
Swiftly the flowers
Are waxing and waning,
The tall yellow iris
Unfolds its corolla
As primroses wither,
Scrolls of fern
Unroll and midges

Dance for an hour
In the evening air,
The brown moth
From its pupa emerges
And the lark's bones
Fall apart in the grass.

The sun that rose
From the sea this morning
Will never return,
For the broadcast light
That brightens the leaves
And glances on water
Will travel tonight
On its long journey
Out of the universe,
Never this sun,
This world, and never
Again this watcher.

THE LOCKED GATES

Everywhere the substance of earth is the gate that we
    cannot pass.
Seek in Hebridean isles lost paradise,
There is yet the heaviness of water, the heaviness of
    stone
And the heaviness of the body I bring to this inviolate place.
Foot sinks in bog as I gather white water-lilies in the
    tarn,
The knee is bruised on rock, and the wind is always
    blowing.
The locked gates of the world are the world's elements,
For the rocks of the beautiful hills hurt, and the silver
    seas drown,
Wind scores deep record of time on the weathered
    boulders,
The bird's hot heart consumes the soaring life to
    feather and bone,
And heather and asphodel crumble to peat that
    smoulders on crofters' fires.

MESSAGE FROM HOME

Do you remember, when you were first a child,
Nothing in the world seemed strange to you?
You perceived, for the first time, shapes already
	familiar,
And seeing, you knew that you had always known
The lichen on the rock, fern-leaves, the flowers of
	thyme,
As if the elements newly met in your body,
Caught up into the momentary vortex of your living
Still kept the knowledge of a former state,
In you retained recollection of cloud and ocean,
The branching tree, the dancing flame.

Now when nature's darkness seems strange to you,
And you walk, an alien, in the streets of cities,
Remember earth breathed you into her with the air,
	with the sun's rays,
Laid you in her waters asleep, to dream
With the brown trout among the milfoil roots,
From substance of star and ocean fashioned you,
At the same source conceived you
As sun and foliage, fish and stream.

Of all created things the source is one,
Simple, single as love; remember
The cell and seed of life, the sphere
That is, of child, white bird, and small blue dragon-fly
Green fern, and the gold four-petalled tormentilla
The ultimate memory.
Each latent cell puts out a future,

Unfolds its differing complexity
As a tree puts forth leaves, and spins a fate
Fern-traced, bird-feathered, or fish-scaled.
Moss spreads its green film on the moist peat,
The germ of dragon-fly pulses into animation and
    takes wing
As the water-lily from the mud ascends on its ropy
    stem
To open a sweet white calyx to the sky.
Man, with farther to travel from his simplicity,
From the archaic moss, fish, and lily parts,
And into exile travels his long way.

As you leave Eden behind you, remember your
    home,
For as you remember back into your own being
You will not be alone; the first to greet you
Will be those children playing by the burn,
The otters will swim up to you in the bay,
The wild deer on the moor will run beside you.
Recollect more deeply, and the birds will come,
Fish rise to meet you in their silver shoals,
And darker, stranger, more mysterious lives
Will throng about you at the source
Where the tree's deepest roots drink from the abyss.

Nothing in that abyss is alien to you.
Sleep at the tree's root, where the night is spun
Into the stuff of worlds, listen to the winds,
The tides, and the night's harmonies, and know
All that you knew before you began to forget,
Before you became estranged from your own being,

Before you had too long parted from those other
More simple children, who have stayed at home
In meadow and island and forest, in sea and river.
Earth sends a mother's love after her exiled son,
Entrusting her message to the light and the air,
The wind and waves that carry your ship, the rain
    that falls,
The birds that call to you, and all the shoals
That swim in the natal waters of her ocean.

Date Due

FEB 1 5 '57			
DEC 1 7 '59			
FEB 7 '60			
MAR 2 1 '61			
DEC 1 8 '70			
	PRINTED	IN U. S. A.	